NORMAL
SEX

For my Mum and Dad
and Nicola

Many thanks to: Ros Badger, Jonathan Boatfield,
Liz Calder, Maryclare Foa, Malcolm Garrett,
Kasper de Graaf, Richard Ingrams, Ben Murphy,
Anita Plank & Kjartan Poskitt

Special thanks to: George Mole (pages 119 - 127),
Pete Bishop (50 & 87), Joe Ewart (35).

Some of these drawings previously appeared
in: Punch, Tatler, Company, Harpers & Queen,
Esquire, The Guardian, The Observer, Blueprint,
Time Out, Skin Two, The Oldie & Blitz.

NORMAL SEX. Copyright © 1993 by Steven Appleby. All
rights reserved. Printed in the United States of America.
No part of this book may be used or reproduced in any
manner whatsoever without written permission except in
the case of brief quotations embodied in critical articles
and reviews. For information address Harper Collins
Publishers, 10 East 53rd Street, New York, NY 10022.

First Harper Collins Edition Published in 1994.

Library of Congress Cataloging in Publication Data
ISBN 0-06-251153-x

94 95 96 97 98 HAD 10 9 8 7 6 5 4 3 2 1

This edition is printed on acid-free paper that meets the
American National Standards Institute 239.48 standard.

NORMAL
SEX

Steven Appleby

HarperSanFrancisco
A Division of HarperCollins*Publishers*

The author and a friend conduct
some essential research.

CONTENTS...

5

Part One

UNDERSTANDING
THE OPPOSITE SEX

FIRST THINGS FIRST

fig 1 – The basic equipment:

A WOMAN   A MAN

Usually one of these is attracted to the other, and vice versa.

Darling...

SIGH...

Some individuals are attracted only to themselves.

Other confused people suspect that they may belong to an as yet undiscovered sex.

I don't know if I'm heterosexual, gay, or...

maybe I'm TRI-SEXUAL!

Of course creepy-crawlies have sexual worries too. Worms have trouble deciding which end is which...

Is this my head?

or this?

which end do I put the condom on?

And amoeba agonise over when to divide.

Is my relationship with myself stable enough for children?

8

Even celestial opposites have doubts about their relationships. Day can't work Night out at all.

He's so gloomy!

But the main thing is not to lose heart. Somewhere there will be a person or object compatible with you no matter how unlikeable, repulsive and unbearable you are.

Will you go out with me?

I'd rather die.

SOME DIFFERENT KINDS OF RELATIONSHIPS:

2 people:

2 people and a friend:

move over!

2 people of the same sex:

2 people of the same sex and a friend:

How do you do...

1 real person and an inflatable person:

Mr. Whipple and Fido:

wheeze...

Good boy.

11

13

when things go wrong
A CAUTIONARY TALE...

Despite all claims to the contrary, the aim in any relationship is for one party to gain the upper hand over the other.

This approach has resulted in many years during which human beings have dominated their environment – but perhaps the balance is about to shift...

An early sign of changes in the status quo:

?

darling?

Not tonight – I have a headache.

Soon other components of the body begin questioning their identities...

hello?   what?

who's there?   ho ho ho ho...

Where?   ssssh!

hup hup hup...   hang on a minute!

Next, inanimate objects prepare to renegotiate their positions...

?   It's good to take the weight off my feet!

oof!!

One moment later:

ah - that's more comfortable...

hmm... yes it is

In this sitting room the T.V. is unhappy with the quality of the viewers.

Huh - think I'll see if there's anything better on the other side...

tea?

coffee?

Here we see Mr. Simpson being treated like a mat by his mat.

Mnnng...

And finally, the table has been turned and is eating the Bingly family off the lino...

CHOMP GUZZLE MUNCH (urp) (Belch) CHOMP SLURP

LOVE

Love is a kind of insanity and people suffering from it should be treated cautiously as they won't listen to a word you say while expecting you to be fascinated by all sorts of far-fetched and implausible stories about someone you probably haven't met and don't want to. Pouring a bucket of water over them is not much use as the madness is too deeply ingrained, but it may make you feel better.

PORTENTS of LOVE:

We all look for help when making a decision - particularly regarding our relationships. Some people read tea leaves, others the stars.

You'll have 60 sons and a daughter...

creak

This lady specialises in interpreting the subtle nuances of a door opening.

While this man bases his entire life on random cloud configurations.

SHE HATES YOU!

SUPERSTITIONS: A small wax doll used to induce love.

The pins represent cupid's arrows...

Here is a useful home-made version of the traditional device for answering the question: "does he, or she, love me – or not?"

a – Cut out all pieces.

b – Glue petals to centre.

c – Fix finished bloom to a pencil with a drawing pin.

d – ask your question while pulling petals off again.

UNREQUITED LOVE.

Love smites all things — but in this case is never consummated due to a lack of communication.

2.

Here both parties remain unfulfilled due to the one-sided nature of their conversation.

3.

In this example communication seems to be taking place but without reaching a happy conclusion.

4. MEANWHILE ON A GRANDER SCALE:

Could millennia of missed opportunities and awkward silences at last be over?

THINGS TO SAY WHEN YOU'RE IN LOVE:

I love you.
You're wonderful.
Yes you really are.
You're marvellous.
I can't believe this
    is happening.
I really do love you.
You're incredible...

PRACTICAL THINGS TO SAY:

Oh, for goodness sake!
Pull yourself together.
Don't be stupid.
Shut up.

THINGS TO THINK:

How long will it last?
Am I deluding myself?
Is she deluding herself?
Does she love me as
    much as I love her?
I can't stop thinking
    about her!
I can't
    sleep.
Aargh!!

PRACTICAL THING TO THINK:

Dum de dum de
    dum dum hum...

MODERN MARRIAGE

GUILT

There's really nothing quite like sex for providing food for guilt of every sort... so it's pointless to feel guilty — unless you get some kind of pleasure out of it.

You disgusting, deceitful, slimeball of a worm-like abhorrent speck!!

You should be ashamed of yourself!

Oh, I am!

Punish me!

A Catholic gets out of the wrong side of the wrong bed.

i - HONEST GUILT

Please forgive me...

please...

ii - DECEITFUL GUILT

I'm not going to admit anything at all!

iii - OVER-REACTING GUILT

I'm going to kill myself and the dog!

Oh no! Not the dog!

iv - DELICIOUS GUILT

my tenth cream horn!

who cares!

With every sexual lie he tells,
The adult Pinocchio's erection swells.

Part Two

PRACTICAL THINGS TO WORRY ABOUT

Squeak
Squeak
squeak...

glug!

PRACTICALITIES

Many people have trouble coping with the reality of sex.
For example, this man keeps it in a little compartment as far away from the rest of his life as possible.

Whatever you do don't go in there!

?

Ugh! Rather hot and squidgy!

Mr Jimjams allows it to fester, forgotten for years on end, in a damp and unhealthy little corner.

Mrs Beelzebub, a lady with firm convictions, pretends that sex doesn't exist so successfully that it doesn't.

I beg your pardon young whatever-you-are!

Wash your mouth out!

Hello miss.

Mr P. – who has rather unusual and amusing needs – tries his hardest to be exactly the same as everyone else.

yes yes. yes. yes

yes

yes

No! er... oops! SYES!!

yes

June F. desperately yearns for a sexual partner even though she knows from past experience that she prefers being out in the garden with a trowel and some bedding plants.

Doctor, I love this pot plant.

Don't be so stupid!

SEX THERAPIST

Teenagers make a mountain out of sex, which they attempt to climb without proper training or safety equipment. Mr Whipple, 67, hasn't even heard of sex. For the past 37 years he has been constructing a full-size replica of the Grand Canyon entirely from matches which eventually he will try to jump on a Harley Davidson made from string.

Help!

Aagh!

Yow!

Damned Kids!

put put put...

Mr Whipple narrowly misses some falling teenagers.

THE SENSITIVE BITS

HONK!

squeeze

A male nightmare.

GROIN HORNS – an evolutionary cul-de-sac in the testicle protection department:

a-

b-

ukkack!

Hug me darling!

Making a mountain out of a molehill...

A USEFUL EASTERN SEXUAL TECHNIQUE:

The Indian Penis Trick.

SEX EDUCATION

Inventing new sexual positions:

a – The Granny Knot.

ow!
oof!
...ouch!

b – The Helicopter.

c – The Steam Train.

Toot!
er...

choo choo...

I can't find the wallpaper brush

d – The Stepladder.

e - The Astronaut.

Roger?

I'm up here, over.

Roger, roger.

f - On the telephone.

Oooh yes...
ooh yes
yes...

g - The In-the-
other-room.

Darling?   Darling?

h - Position 96
(in which you both
get to go to
sleep).

AN EXTRACT FROM 'THE BORING SEX GUIDE' (Volume 4)

POSITION 36:
Move part A up to part B, then in a motion B, C, D, E, (repeat). Raise foot F and place against part G. Make expression 3(c) (see page 409). Say: "Oh yes, darling."

fig A   fig B   Book

P.T.O.

AN EXTRACT FROM 'THE ENCYCLOPAEDIA OF SEXUAL POSITIONS & DEVIATIONS': MONOGAMY.

z z z z z z z z z

SEXUAL TECHNIQUE - some erogenous zones and some erroneous zones.

A few of the 600 or so penis erogenous zones:

a-   b-

c-   d-

e-   f-

g-   h- →a+B=

$\sqrt{100}x$

FOOT FUN!
Specific parts of the foot correspond to parts of the body - see chart below.

PRESS (Buckles & poppers)

FUMBLE (Buttons)

SCRATCH (apologise)

PULL (zipper)

SQUEEZE (Top)

TICKLE (Difficult clasp)

A device for arousing some internal erogenous zones:

Pants down!   er...

Manipulating the little-known tongue erogenous zones:

a   B

c

f   d   e

Mnnng...

AN ORGY

39

A GUIDE TO ORGASMS:

Raaaaaaaah...

i - method acting.

a... a... a...

ii - Character acting.

Uh-hurrrr...

iii - Improvisation.

Yaaaaah...

iv - Socialite.

I'm sorry?

Have you finished?

I wasn't paying attention...

v - Long-term partner.

Oh.
Yes.
Ah.

Thank you.

vi - Polite.

HOME SEX THERAPIST:

For those who can't climax, here is a foolproof way to reach orgasm. The special chart below (Patent Applied For But Laughed at) will, when read from start (point a) to finish (point z) result in a fully satisfactory experience induced by eye muscle movement alone. Attractively designed to look good in a frame by the bed for emergency use.

If YOUR sex life is boring, why not add a little spice with one of these non-toxic SEX TOYS...

A vibrating Something-or-other. Available in flesh colour (dead) or purple. Batteries not included.

A superb whatsit - and good value at the moment - HURRY while stocks last! Blue only.

A large washable thingy - One size only.

A set of 3 edible what-do-you-call-its. Just what the doctor would order if he knew!

A realistic doo-dah - in presentation case. Instructions enclosed.

SPECIAL OFFER

Glow-in-the-dark 'His 'n' Hers' TM underwear! Putting out the lights won't extinguish the passion! Now you can find one another in the dark! Guaranteed...

CONTRACEPTION

A WARNING!

43

ASSORTED CONDOM
DESIGNS:

Cute NOVELTY ANIMAL CONDOMS:

THE 'CATAMARAN'
A novelty condom...
Presumably.

a.

b.

c.

MEASURING
CONDOM - up
to 1000 cc.

AN EDIBLE CONDOM:

available in brown, white
or granary.
  WARNING - on its own
  does not constitute
  a balanced diet -
  must be supplemented
  by beer and snacks.

KNITTED WOOLLEN CONDOM:

If it was good enough for your Grandad, blah blah blah...

A present from Grandma (who had fifteen children).

TOTAL PROTECTION:

mmmmmg?*

The complete body condom.

*Shall we go to bed darling?

THE 'OPTIMIST'

FINALLY ~ A special condom approved by the Pope for Roman Catholics:

the HOLY Condom. praise him!

Learning how to put on a condom using various vegetables and household items:

A TURNIP.

A LETTUCE.

A TELEPHONE.

A GRAPE.

We'll need two.

A CAR.

AN UNFORTUNATE MIX-UP AT THE RUBBER PRODUCTS FACTORY.

ALTERNATIVES to the CONDOM

fig a ~

NO!

fig b ~ Reading a good book.

Darling?.. Ssssh!

fig c ~ A double chastity belt.

This is exciting!

So naughty yet ineffectual!

A NEW KIND OF BIRTH CONTROL

Homing sperm.

SAFE SEX

Safe sex using imagination alone to achieve satisfaction:

MODERN NEUROSIS:

Pre-Sex sterilisation.

52

An embarrassing adhesive moment caused by a build-up of static electricity:

I'm terribly sorry - are you wearing nylon?

Darling... mmmm?..

True Love - Mr Balloon meets his future wife during a brief career as a Christmas decoration.

54

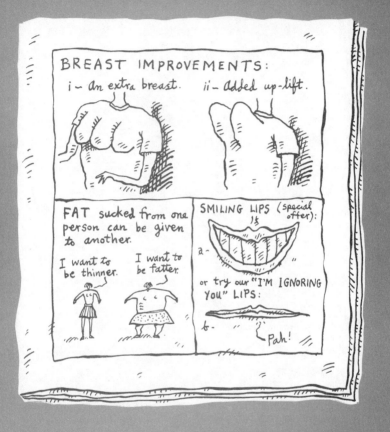

After you, darling!
The 'de Sade Brothers' tummy trimmer is a real blessing in today's home!
PATENT APPLIED FOR (BUT DENIED)

59

SUGGESTED NOSES:

a-   b-

c - A philosophical nose.

A pair of Eskimo inspired 'His-n-Hers' creations.

The Staircase.

d - 'Le Valet'

A practical nose for hanging coats on.

ouch!

e - The Door Stop.

PENIS ADJUSTMENT & CUSTOMISING —
Choose from one of these stock designs, or alternatively our engineers will work from your own drawings and sketches.

FISHNET SHEATH.

COLLAR (with identity disc).

TOUPEE.

'GO-FASTER' STRIPES.

FURRY DICE.

STILLETTO BOOT.

SMART MISSILE.

ROLLS ROYCE.

THE SHERLOCK

SPRINKLER

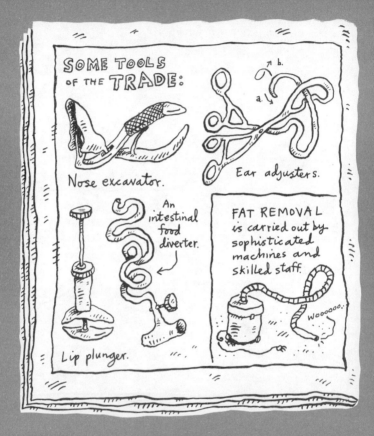

SOME TOOLS OF THE TRADE:

Nose excavator.

Ear adjusters.

a. b.

An intestinal food diverter.

Lip plunger.

FAT REMOVAL is carried out by sophisticated machines and skilled staff.

Woooooo...

WHAT SATISFIED
CUSTOMERS HAVE
SAID:

Thank you,
'Bob's'

Thank
you,
'Bob's'

Thank you,
'Bob's'

Why not apply for Bob's credit
card and pay for your
restorative surgery at inflated
interest rates
over a vague
and not clearly
specified length
of time?

'Bob's'
FRANCHISE
A.N. OTHER SUCKER

63

After your course in plastic surgery a healthy-looking tan is just the thing — but follow these tips to avoid premature aging and skin cancer!

TANNING GUIDE:
a useful chart.

A SPECIAL OUTFIT
FOR DECORATIVE
TANNING:

1989:
Before →
after →

1999:
Before →
after →

tanning bag:
(baste frequently)

a - BEFORE.

b - DURING.

c - AFTER.

64

DECORATIVE SHAVING.

Taking inspiration from the topiary in some of our great ornamental gardens, imaginative clipping can add amusement and interest to an otherwise dull and lack-lustre sex life. Try these at home (or outside if you prefer).

Hairspray and careful tending have resulted in THE QUIFF:

PUBIC PORTRAITS:

i -

ii -

iii -

Winston Churchill.   Mother Theresa.   D.H. Lawrence.

POETIC MOMENTS:

Butterflies hovering over apple blossom on a hot summer's afternoon.

Lion cub lapping at the edge of a pool at dawn.

F1-11 cruising at 15,000 feet stalked by a MIG.

DRESSING UP

Before baring your all, you need to impress with your attire. Carefully chosen clothing can work wonders by concealing the uglier, wobblier parts and highlighting the occasional pleasing bit.

THE EMPEROR'S NEW CLOTHES...

I think I preferred the invisible suit I didn't see earlier...

fabulous...

The invisible suit turns out to be the best of a bad lot.

CLOTHES TO BE SEEN IN IN...

A RUBBERIST –

I'm erasing!

BOOB TUBES –

with magnifying lenses!

SKIN TIGHT –

That _IS_ my skin!

SKIMPY – Oops - I forgot to put anything on at all!

THONG

THING

THONGY-THING

Three nudists wearing clothes.

TRYING OUT CORSETS:

Breast corsets.

waist corset.

Leg corset.

Gaaaak!

neck corset (short lived).

Penis corset

EXPERIMENTING with a porcupine suit:

Big hug!

Seen here concealed beneath street clothes:

Hello Vicar.

70

Part Three

IMPRACTICAL THINGS TO WORRY ABOUT

More and more people these days enjoy a good, healthy fetish.

Roger and Gillian X, for example, enjoy drinking cups of tea off each other's bodies — are they abnormal?

A rural man who prefers to remain anonymous, gets pleasure from dressing as a lettuce, being watered, thinned out and re-potted in the greenhouse.

cover me in French dressing!

It's getting a bit dark in here.

Mr. P from Herne Hill likes dressing as a bedside lamp and being turned on.

74

Reading is an interest which many people develop, and David L — dressed as a large wasp — chews his copy of

BUZZ...

The Times into a paste and uses it to wallpaper his room.

But some people go too far! In the interest of public decency we simply cannot print a picture of the perverts who derive some sort of disturbed pleasure from the wearing of brightly coloured nylon sportswear.

A DOUBLE PERVERSION

A man, dressed as a woman, dressed as a man.

HOW DOES IT START?

Here we see that some sexual fetishes grow from experiences rooted in early childhood...

No more ice cream!

AGE 7   AGE 30

Eat your greens!

goo...

AGE 7   AGE 30

Do your homework

AGE 7   AGE 30

THE BUTTOCKHEADS

Caught out by his wife in a minor misdemeanour, Mr Buttockhead indulges in a predictably conventional sexual fantasy.

Spank my face!

THE EFFECT IN LATER LIFE OF BANNING CANING IN SCHOOLS:

you naughty boy!

Write me a letter of apology and 200 lines!

oh yes! yes!

Save on electricity with a 'HOOVERIST' –
the useful side of fetishism.

This top-of-
the-range
model picks
up cat hairs
and shampoos
the
carpet!

Whoooooo
er
es
er
on
ee

Mr Hetherington-Fotherington is a peer of
the realm and rather expensive.

This 'HIS-N-HERS' tongue clamp is essential for the couple who appreciate the exquisite subtlety of being unable to kiss.

Furniture fetishists:

Two Santa Claus
fetishists:

A jug (or genie)
fetishist:

A CAR FETISHIST
POLISHING:

TWO SCRABBLE
PLAYERS:

FOOD AND FETISHISM:

You've had your cake, Simon - now go make your bed and lie in it!

FOOD & FOOTWEAR: exotic sexual appetites can sometimes be satisfied with shoes made out of pastry, chocolate and fresh cream.

1:

2:

SPLUDGE!

DON'T WORRY
if you've got a
FOOD FETISH
You're not peculiar —
everyone else has one too!

Everyone except
me, of course!

You
perverts!

Ha ha
ha

Don't be embarrassed if you
feel the urge to dress as a
rubber glove and splash about
in a huge sink full of giant
crockery.

It's quite natural to wear a carrot suit and climb into an enormous steamer.

You should be boiled to within an inch of your life!

Steaming is the modern way!

Gregory likes to pollinate rhubarb ~ so far with a sad lack of success.

I must write to Gardeners' Question Time...

RHUBARB PATCH

Roger, who has had a sex
change to 'IT', now
reproduces like a seedless
grape.

Um...

How is
that,
exactly?..

But some people feel compelled
to eat only vegetables,
which is a bit weird. Try
to be tolerant...

Do you get some sort of
sick pleasure
out of
it?

A
healthy
pleasure,
actually.
La la la...

COOKING & SEX

Why not try improvising a sauce for the body using ingredients readily to hand in your kitchen. How about a Welsh Rarebit inspired concoction, or a Banana Custard, perhaps? Delicious hot (not TOO hot) or cold (not TOO cold).

mmmg... delicious... um...

Don't talk with your mouth full!

ETIQUETTE TIP — Using a knife and fork is considered bad manners.

LESSER-KNOWN FOOD APPRECIATION SOCIETIES:

The donut club.

Stilletto glasses.

A PERVERSE FLY:

the SEX LIFE of MACHINES

i — One day machines will learn how to reproduce.

Avert your eyes from the kitchen, dears!

Aw...

CLANK
CLUNK
Rattle
CLINK
THUD
Bump...

But I like watching the cooker and the fridge!

90

ii ~ Cross breeding will produce
some curious hybrids...

These fridge/cookers are a bit
                disappointing...

My ice-cream
is soft!

my pie is
raw!

iii ~ ...and some machines will
develop curious perversions:

The toaster has started
dressing up as a
            table
            lamp!

iv ~ When machine relationships
turn sour, everyone suffers.

The fridge
has moved
out of
the
kitchen
for a
trial
period.

v ~ Finally, an unforeseen
consequence:

Dad's with
the fridge
again.
First it
was the T.V.
now
this!

you make
me feel
young!

BUZZ

SEXUAL TABOOS ～ No. 1

Having sex with a dead
person.

SEXUAL TABOOS ~ No. 2

ANIMALS.

A horse lover.
(The British are well-known
dog and cat lovers, too.)

SEXUAL TABOOS ~ No. 3

DEATH.

HEADS WILL ROLL!

Ahem - Darling, I'd like a divorce.

Mr Praying Mantis makes a novel suggestion.

Part Four

THE JOY OF
STAYING SINGLE

LIVING
ON YOUR OWN

Being single is the perfect relationship. You get to spend twenty-four hours a day with the person you know and love best in the world, and of whose companionship you never tire.

I think I'll do exactly what I want today, then exactly what I want again after that, then...

I love me,
I love me not.
I love me,
I love me not
I...

A well-adjusted single person can generally cope with living alone without falling prey to obscure religious cults, fluffy-pet-obsession or hallucinations. And he or she will soon be able to bask in the envious glances of various married friends.

Life begins when you're single.

THE POSITIVE SIDE.

THE NEGATIVE SIDE.

Party time at Mr Unpopular's house.

No. 1 in a series of
USEFUL THINGS to say to
a persistent admirer:

SEX WITH YOURSELF

Things to say to yourself in a solo relationship:

Not tonight - I'm washing my hair.

Are you having an affair with a real person?

I'm too tired. Maybe tomorrow...

PROPS & DEVICES for the devotee of solo sex:

A portable motion-powered orifice for day-long comfort.

A USEFUL CHAIR:

hello

A THIRD ARM:

(clockwork mechanism)

A cup of tea and some chunks of chocolate.

AN INFLATABLE PERSON:

"Wash behind your ears"

Shown here is the Ann Winter's inflatable public school matron. (No orifices whatsoever.)

A CUDDLING MACHINE:

There there...
There there...

CHUG
CHUG
CHUG
CHUG
CHUG...

Buying a solo sex machine.

SEX EDUCATION –
Some positions for solo sex:

i – Sitting down.

Splendid

ii – Lying down.

comfy!

iii – Standing up.

Yes
indeedy

iv – Hanging upside
down from the
bannisters.

Er... now hang
on a
minute...

THE SIDE EFFECTS –

Going blind:

Who me?

What
rubbish!

Insanity:

I'm going to
go and watch
soaps on T.V.

APPENDICES

Men the Truth

They conceal their emotions.

MEN ②
THE TRUTH

They go bald.

They all like sport.

MEN 13
THE TRUTH

Size is unimportant.

They have a flair for cooking.

They buy practical clothing
for their loved ones.

113

MEN ⑯

THE TRUTH

They get iller than anyone else.

They are experts with machinery.

They feel like sandpaper.

They make good fathers.

The side effect of sex can be children, who in turn grow up and have more children, and so on. This is something to do with the Meaning of Life.

FEMINIST NIGHTMARE

APPENDIX III
Courtship & Reproduction on Other Planets

Let us take an absorbing and educational look into the private affairs and marital arrangements of some typical galactic inhabitants.

WARNING – Some people may find the following material offensive while others, if they have tentacles, more than two heads and strange clusters of sexual organs, could well be led astray by the arousing drawings and erotic text.

uh oh – looks like we're about to have sex.

Buzzzzzzzzz zzzzzzzz

Plant People of Nimbos having a lie-in.

The universal language of Love.

CHEMICAL ADULTERY - an element arrives
home to discover that his gaseous entity
has formed a compound with the
liquid next door.

A short-sighted
Lardat finds he
has eloped with a
stone.

Spheres making music.

GENITALS of the UNIVERSE:

I'm sure it went here last time...

How about over here?

This complex and puzzling apparatus creates problems for the folk of Lego V.

Even the owners of this impressive item don't know exactly what to do with it.

We're almost extinct!

Actually I'm the genitals and he's the person

The inhabitants of Glower make fine underarm bowlers thanks to skills developed during their curious method of reproduction.

This rather boring method of reproduction is the sad lot that has fallen to the rotarians.

It's so small!

Evolution has played a cruel trick on the gentle folk of Planet Percy.

Two residents of Gelding 4 discover that they possess no reproductive apparatus whatsoever.

(yawn.)

?

FINALLY - Birth...

Waaaaah!

The ever-hungry Blutton - a
creature less good-natured than
the stork - is responsible for
delivering the babies on
Planet Mopsy.

APPENDIX IV

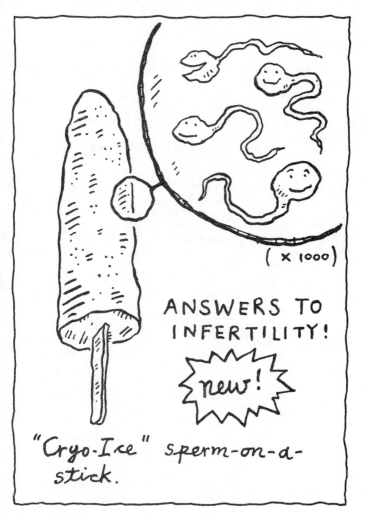

(× 1000)

ANSWERS TO
INFERTILITY!

new!

"Cryo-Ice" sperm-on-a-
stick.